The Silly Side of Sixty

Jennifer Green

ISBN-13: 978-1507777213

ISBN-10: 1507777213

DEDICATION

To my best friends - you know who you are -
who had my poems inflicted on them,
but still managed to laugh in the right places!

CONTENTS

STILL ROCKING & ROLLING

If you'd have told me at twenty
What the future held for me,
And that I'd still be rocking
At the age of seventy-three,

I'd have smiled and I'd have humoured you:
At that age? Are you mad?
But reality's been good to me
And I'm still singing with the band.

We were legends in the sixties,
Famous for our rocking sessions,
Now the kids have never heard of us,
Except in history lessons.

We tour the UK cities,
We still can pack them in,
Though our audience is diminishing
And the crowds are rather thin.

We're not mobbed as we used to be,
The atmosphere is not the same,
As the audience comes tottering
On their ubiquitous Zimmer frames.

Now we're all oldies together,
All of a certain age:
Pensioners in the audience
And pensioners on the stage.

We'd love to sing some new songs,
But the fans have made it clear,
The ones that they remember,
Are the ones they want to hear.

So we belt out our one-hit wonder,
As if we didn't mind
That we're singing this old classic
For the twenty-thousandth time.

We rock as good as ever,
You would not believe our age,
And we keep our public happy,
Till we stagger off the stage.

*****

THE NAKED LADY

There's a naked lady in the window
But it's not a mortal sin,
For the window is a dress shop
And she's just a mannequin!

THE SUPERMARKET QUEUE

(or Keep Me Waiting at Your Peril !!!)

I'm in a hurry and I'm waiting
In a supermarket line.
I only wanted one small thing
And I haven't got the time

To hang around while someone
Is fumbling for their purse.
I'm spitting mad and hissing bricks
And trying not to curse . . . . [out loud!]

So I mumble to the person
Stood behind me in the queue,
About the lack of open checkouts
And staff who've disappeared from view.

And I will never ever patronise
This branch ever again,
Though 'we aim to serve you right'
Is what they might decide to claim.

I'm going to talk to someone,
The manager no less,
To complain about the service or the lack of it
And for causing me such stress.

Now I'm ranting and I'm raving,
I will tell them what I think:
I'm an irritated customer
About to make a stink!

When I finally hit the till-point,
I know exactly what I'll say,
Then I'm told " *Thank you for waiting*"
And I meekly walk away . . . . . .

*****

CHEAP DRINK

I just bought a six-pack,
You'll think I shouldn't oughta,
But before you start to censure me,
I'll confess that it was water!

CONCENTRATION

Now I'm really going to concentrate,
No hesitation and no doubt,
But I'm only halfway through this verse
And my mind's gone walkabout.

I can concentrate at lectures,
But only for a minute;
The subject is so interesting,
But my heart just isn't in it.

The lecturer is crystal clear
And I listen very hard.
The subject is so down-to-earth,
But my brain is up round Mars,

Yet as someone was to mention,
I appear to pay attention.
Though ask me something and you'll find,
I've left reality behind.

This poem would be longer,
But you've probably guessed what,
My mind has started wandering
And now I've really lost the plot!

THE OLD BAG

I'm taking the old bag shopping
And much to my surprise,
She may look rather old and fragile,
But she can carry a lot of supplies.

She appears rather wrinkled and crumpled,
She's certainly seen better days,
But I'll buy lots more stuff,
And keep loading her up,
For she's useful in other small ways.

I've taken her all over the world, you see.
I once took her to Spain for a bet.
Though her shopping days may be numbered,
There's still life in the old bag yet!

*****

A BARGAIN?

The shop has incredible offers,
With bargains you wouldn't believe!
But does twenty per cent off,
Not the price, but the stock,
Mean the sweater has only one sleeve?

FOOD SHOPPING

I'm careful when I shop for food,
I have to make sure that it's right,
And the supermarket offers no quick fix;
I may still be there at midnight.

The vast array of food is daunting,
Not sure I know where to begin,
So I'll concentrate on the things I need most,
Plan it out like a military campaign.

I've checked where the food has come from,
And if it's a country that I support,
Then I'm happy to buy it regularly,
Not just as a last resort.

I worry about the air miles
And the distance that it's travelled.
If I don't buy goods that are locally sourced,
Will the whole world become unravelled?

I've checked the list of contents
To make sure that I can see
That all the ingredients listed
Appear to agree with me.

I've looked up all the E-numbers
And they seem to be benign,
But all these complicated decisions
Take up lots and lots of time.

I've checked that it's organic
Though that may not be a must
And if they say it's vegetarian,
I'll have to take that one on trust.

Then what about the calories?
And is it high on fat?
If it contains too much preservative,
Then I'm not too keen on that.

Now there's one thing that's eluding me
And it means you'll have to wait,
While I search everywhere on the packet
For that illusive sell-by date.

Is it on the bottom?
Or maybe at the top?
Or has it disappeared completely
As if someone's rubbed it off?

Make sure that the tin isn't dented
Or the packet doesn't look split.
Did I end up with what I intended
Or miss the one vital thing on my list?

This obsession with every detail,
Has taken me far too long
And when I unpack the stuff that I've bought,
I find that I've still got it wrong!

*****

THE COUPON

It was just a little coupon,
It could save me 50p,
But you wouldn't believe the anxiety.
This piece of paper had in store for me.

First I had to find it again;
I had seen it when I browsed.
It moved from the page where I spotted it;
That shouldn't be allowed!

Then I had to remind myself,
To clip it from the magazine.
The scissors had gone walkabout,
So I tore out the page I'd seen.

Then I had to remember
To take it with me when I shopped.
I could easily have forgotten it,
When to the store I popped.

So I found the product on the shelf,
Check the details carefully as I choose it,
Reached the till with the coupon close at hand
And then forgot to use it!

*****

CHAOS IN THE CAR PARK
. . . . and in store!

It's Friday at the supermarket
Everyone's gone shopping mad,
The car park is in chaos,
Only a few spaces to be had.

Cars are streaming through the entrance
Turning when you least expect it.
You wish that they would just reverse
And head home via the exit.

Cars are circling ever nearer
As they're trying to regroup.
I swear I've seen that one before
Heading round another loop.

Cars cling bumper to bumper
Searching for that one elusive space,
So the drivers can disgorge themselves
And join the trolley race.

Grab a trolley from the rack
And head into the store,
Dodge between careering cars
As the battle lines are drawn.

For if the cars aren't out to get you
Then the trolleys surely will.
They're belting up the aisles
And rushing for the tills.

A fully laden trolley
Is a missile in disguise.
The speed it heads in your direction
Will take you by surprise.

The aggressiveness of trolley pushers
Really starts to rankle
And if I don't keep my wits about me
They'll jab me in the ankle.

With my one small basket
I just don't have a hope
To infiltrate the trolley lines
With which the aisles are choked.

So I'll dodge the bulging trolleys
And see if I can win
With only a basket to protect me
I'm sure I can just cut in.

There are two old ladies chatting
And they're blocking up the shelf.
They're too engrossed in conversation
To think of anybody else.

And when I say "Excuse me"
They take it as an insult
And I end up apologising
As though it were my fault.

Never mind the children bawling
Demanding more and more,
Not content with being vocal
They throw groceries on the floor.

I slalom in and out of trolleys,
Grab things written on my list,
But with this gridlock queue of shoppers,
There'll be something that I've missed.

All I want is to shop in peace
But I'm hemmed in by the trolleys.
There was something else I wanted
But now I can't be bothered.

With twenty-four hour opening
They could pick another time.
So why must they all descend on the store
At the exact same moment that I am?

I've battled my way through all this jam
But getting out could be worse.
I'll have to brave the queues at checkout
. . . . . but that's another verse!

*****

OH NO . . . . !!

There's this really crummocky person,
In a shop window reflection I've seen;
A crazy old bat
In a pink woolly hat
And I'm thinking, oh lordy, it's me!

AT THE THEATRE

ACT ONE

The lights are dimmed, the stage is set,
I'm feeling all a quiver;
Anticipating what's to come,
But from the audience, there's a whisper.

Perhaps this audible interaction
Isn't too much a distraction,
As the band begins to play the opening tune.
And don't get too downhearted
The show has not quite started
And they're bound to shut up talking fairly soon.

There's someone sitting next to me,
Who's really not that slim,
And he's spilling over on my seat
As I'm squirming to fit in.

And someone tall in front of me,
Though this is nothing new.
I'm rocking side to side to see.
Could I claim 'restricted view'?

And you can bet there's someone coughing,
Not a elegant splutter, but a hacking loud
guffaw.
You'd think that they were dying,
But before you end up crying,
Just get them booted out the exit door.

INTERVAL

There's the people right behind you
That bash into your seat,
And the ones that squeeze in front of you
And tread upon your feet.

There's the picnics and the ice-cream,
That nearly end up in your lap,
And the lemonade that soon may be
Cascading down your back.

ACT TWO

Now the action's really gripping,
You could almost hear a pin,
But there's still some more distractions,
With my patience wearing thin.

There's a sweet paper rustling somewhere
And the noise is loud enough,
But they're trying to do it slowly -
Just hurry up and rip it off!

Oh, never mind the sweeties,
Never mind the coughs,
Now a mobile phone is ringing
And I've really had enough!

AFTERWARDS

So why go to the theatre?
Why put up with all this hell,
When I could stay home and watch telly
And be entertained just as well?

But the actors hold me spellbound,
And the staging was unique,
The plot was so exciting
And I'm tapping to the beat.

And when the show has ended
And applause begins to roar,
The atmosphere's electric
And I want to shout 'Encore'.

Despite the mumbling and the moaning,
It's really been a treat,
And my heart trips much more lightly,
As I head off down the street.

*****

COME FOR COFFEE

I asked her round for coffee,
Just a casual drink and chat,
But now she thinks we're bosom pals
And not content with that . . .

She's asked me round for coffee
And I expect I'll have to go,
Though I don't want another friendship,
I haven't the heart to say "No".

Then I'll have to invite her back again.
Now I'm starting to feel frightened.
She might think this is all great fun,
To carry on ad infinitum . . .

*****

DE-CLUTTERING

I'm having a good de-clutter,
Taking books to the charity store,
Making some space on my bookshelves,
So I can go out and buy a few more!

*****

THE PERFECT GUEST

The perfect guest arrives on time,
Proffering flowers and a bottle of wine.
Then asks how I am and doesn't mind,
When I tell him in detail about my decline.

He's a lovely man to have around,
So considerate and polite,
And never seems to get too tired
Of watching home movies late at night.

I took him out to dinner,
He was happy to pick up the tab.
I admit I felt slightly guilty,
But really not all that bad.

He used his car to take me round
To meetings and to church,
And I know I can rely on him,
Not to leave me in the lurch.

We shopped for food together,
Stocking up wasn't hard,
And by the time we reached the checkout,
He'd whipped out his credit card.

He found out it was my birthday,
(I just happened to let it slip!),
So he organised a party,
With balloons and cake and chips.

He asked if he could help at all -
Was there something he could do?
So he ended up painting the ceiling
And fixing the broken loo.

When it came to the gardening,
He was pleased to lend a hand.
The weeds had taken over,
Now it looks pristine and grand.

The family descended without warning,
It wasn't part of the plan,
But he said he would be delighted,
To share his bedroom with some of the clan.

Soon the perfect guest departed,
I was sad to see him go.
He said he'd love to come again,
In another year or so.

I wrote several times to invite him back,
Made sure my intentions were clear,
But I never heard from him again;
He simply disappeared . . . .

*****

DON'T TELL ME!

I'm a sympathetic listener,
Sometimes it gets me in a mess,
When I may be in a hurry
And I want to hear a little less.

It seems like every passing stranger
With a pressing need to chat,
Heads right in my direction
And I'm getting tired of that.

Then the hotel receptionist
Tells me her life is full of doom,
When all I want is to grab the key
And head off to my room.

On the bus, a stranger sits down
On the seat right next to me
And tells me her life story
Which she's eager I should heed.

I'm really not that interested
But I nod and hum and sigh.
All I want is to look out the window
As the countryside passes by.

On the street, I met a lady
Who wouldn't let me go,
Before she'd related her whole medical history,
Which I didn't want to know.

You may think I'm unsociable
And with that I would agree,
So when you've a trivial thought you feel the
need to share,
Find another stranger somewhere
And please DON'T TELL ME!

*****

MY GEORGIAN HOUSE

It's very nice to chat to you.
What shall we talk about?
There's a subject that's very dear to me -
My small Georgian townhouse.

I bought it as a 'blank canvas',
So I'm gradually doing it up.
I'm tackling most of the work on my own;
It's engrossing and frustrating stuff.

It takes up an awful lot of my time,
Researching to make it authentic.
With eight or so rooms, to decorate and fill,
I need quite a bit of incentive.

I've papered the walls and painted the ceilings,
I've fixed all the coving myself.
I'm now quite a master, at painting pilasters
And moving around the odd shelf.

There are table lamps and wall lights.
I've done all the wiring to boot.
The lighting was tricky, the wallpaper sticky,
But I've acquired useful skills I can use.

I buy Georgian-style furniture when I find it;
It's much harder than it would seem.
My granddaughter enjoys changing everything
round,
So it won't end up like a museum.

The stairs have been carpeted, curtains are
hung,
The kitchen's well kitted and neat,
And I've just started tackling the ballroom,
The wood flooring should look a real treat.

I buy odd ornaments when I find them,
Making sure that the scale is right.
And now that the chandeliers are in place,
It looks stunning when lit up at night.

It's a labour of love, it costs a small fortune,
But all of the pleasures outweigh
The hassle and worry, for the sense of
discovery,
Makes the learning curve fun, every day.

I can see from your face that you're really quite
envious.
Come round and see the final effect.

Oh I know you'll be incredibly impressed with my
dolls house -
Is that not what you thought that I meant?

*****

ON THE TRAIL OF ART NOUVEAU

My friend and I have a passion for buildings,
We enjoy them wherever we go,
But senses start reeling, eyes hit the ceiling,
On the trail of art nouveau.

We're optimistic and travel with hope,
Our mental enthusiasm to nourish.
There's a joy in finding curling forms,
Ending in a spectacular flourish.

We've ambled in Antwerp and loitered in Lille,
In Brussels we browsed for days.
Lots of buildings in Nancy have taken our fancy,
In so many quirky old ways.

It's not that we actually like the style,
Though we appreciate all that we see.
For when art nouveau becomes trendy
And the architecture looks bendy,

It all depends on degree.

We respond to other interesting buildings,
Anything that brings a smile to our sight,
So our thoughts also echo, with a bit of art deco
And a generous dose of Lloyd Wright.

So next time you see two old biddies,
Oohing and aahing down the road,
It may very well be, just my best friend and me,
On the search for more art nouveau.

*****

THE CLEANING BLUES

I once did a bit of cleaning,
Though it wasn't even spring!
But there's so much else to distract me;
I don't want to miss out on a thing.

I've watched programmes on the TV,
Where the people seem so sad,
As the dust and possessions accumulate,
So maybe I'm not really that bad,

For I can still see the pattern of the carpet,
I can swing the proverbial cat.
I know that my house isn't perfect,
But I'm just going to leave it at that!

*****

LOST BOOK

There's a book I want to look at,
I have a copy on my shelf,
But now I just can't find it
And for that I blame myself.

I know where it should be lurking
With the others I can see
And I'm frustrated I can't find it
In the place it's meant to be.

I can see it in my mind's eye
I know the colour and the size.
It was definitely paperback
Or a hardback in disguise.

When did I last have it?
Try and give my brain a yank,
But the answer is alluding me
And my mind has drawn a blank!

I remember reading it recently,
Then I put it somewhere safe,
Amongst other similar subjects.
Maybe that was my mistake.

For if I'd replaced it in the bookcase
in the place that it would fit,
I wouldn't be wasting all this time
In searching round for it.

So I skim the nearby shelving
And the cupboard by the door
And the pile of miscellaneous tomes
That's accumulated on the floor.

Then I look in the study
I know it's definitely not there.
Maybe I removed it earlier
And have taken it upstairs.

When I last had a clear-out
Did I take it to the charity store?
Perhaps I lent it to a friend
Or the neighbour from next door.

I've searched every nook and cranny
In boxes and cupboards I've looked.
I've wasted hours and I'm frazzled,
For my patience was never that good.

Eureka! I have found it,
I can put this frustration to rest.
It's hiding, in full view, on the shelf,
In the place I began this quest!

*****

GARDENING

When I plant something new in the garden
There's never any surprise;
It may blossom apace
Take up far too much space
Or otherwise curl up and die!

*****

THE LETTER

Thanks for your letter received in the post,
I'm acknowledging with some distress.
Though you sent it in pristine condition,
It arrived in a bit of a mess.

It had obviously been dunked in some water
And when it was thoroughly wet,
It was all screwed up and mangled
And arrived looking very upset.

The envelope designed to protect it,
Didn't stand much of a chance,
With a few rips and tears on the outside,
It's appearance was not much enhanced.

Surprisingly when it was opened
The contents were all intact,
Though the cheque was decidedly crumpled
And the note was stuck to the back.

At least it was dry when it reached me,
That's one point to count in its favour,
And the address was just about legible,
So it managed to reach this safe haven.

I feel sorry for this small epistle,
It didn't deserve this sad fate.
The Society for the Prevention of Cruelty to
Letters
Has been thought up a little too late.

*****

OLD FRIENDS

It's lovely when you meet someone
Walking down the street
A chance encounter, time to chat
Pleased to find someone to greet.

I bumped into a man today
And as the conversation grew,
We stood and talked for ages
Like old friends often do.

We talked about the weather
We talked about the past,
We talked about the little things
In life we hate the most.

And how we both loathe Christmas
And bank holidays as well,
Then the lovely town we live in
And in which we love to dwell.

And the film that I had seen last week
And he had seen it too,
And we both agreed the plot was difficult
To work out who was who!

And the parking problem's dreadful
So friends don't come that often,
And the shops that keep on closing -
We seemed to have so much in common.

I was sad when we parted
But then got in a 'tizz';
Though we must be really good old friends,
I can't remember who he is!

He may have been a stranger,
Looked like someone else I know,
Or maybe he just recognised me
From somewhere long ago.

But chances are when he gets home,
I'll bet you a whole fiver,
He'll think about it long and hard
And won't have a clue who I was either!

*****

ANY DAY WILL DO

Let's meet up for coffee,
Any day will do,
Though not this week, I'm busy,
But you could suggest a date or two.

Next Monday isn't looking good,
I'll be out all day, you see.
Tuesday's problematic too,
And I need to keep it free.

Then I'll be away for several days,
So the following week is out.
Then there are various appointments,
I'd forgotten all about.

The week after, I'll be in and out,
Though more likely out than in,
But maybe I can re-arrange things
To try and squeeze you in.

But not the following Thursday,
And the 5th and 6th are looking busy,
March and April are reserved for trips.
Free time? There just isn't any.

Retirement is so hectic
And any day you choose,
There's always something going on,
So much I've booked to do.

Now how about six weeks on Friday?
I'm definitely clear for the whole day.
Oh no, it's such a pity,
That's when you'll be away.

But I'd so *love* to get together,
Catch up on all your news,
And I'm really very flexible.
Yes, nearly any day will do!

*****

THE COMMITTEE

There's a local charity you feel sorry for,
But beware of taking pity,
For before you have time to turn around,
You'll be 'volunteered' for the committee.

It's a great boost to be asked to join them,
You'll feel really proud of yourself,
But beware of the metaphorical arm up your
back -
They've already tried everyone else!

It looks like a solid agenda,
The secretary's pen is poised,
But what looks impressive on paper,
In reality, fills a great void.

The committee forms a repository
For lost souls with nothing to do,
They take great delight spending hours
And never come to a majority view.

Decisions aren't made at committee,
For the members never agree
About what it says in their constitution,
Or even about who should make tea.

Remember at every meeting
To keep your opinions quiet,
Or you'll end up running the whole dam thing,
It'll start taking over your life.

You begin as an ordinary member,
And you're proud when you are promoted
To an officer of the committee,
Where you'll always be outvoted.

It sounds so good on your CV,
To say you're chairman of the so-and-so.
Anyone ignorant of committees is impressed -
You'll get grins from those in the know.

For they've had their fill of committees
And it's not that easy to resign.
They'll swear blind they can't find a replacement,
No-one else seems to have any time.

So if someone should slyly ask you
If you have any time that's free,
Just hand them a fiver, say you're really a
skiver:
Ask anyone, other than me!

There's just one small word to remember,
If you're ever tempted to stray,
Wherever you go, rehearse the word 'NO'
Or you'll live to regret it one day!

*****

CHARITY BEGINS ...

I took a few things to the charity shop,
But got rather carried away
And regretting my hasty decision,
Bought them back the following day!

*****

THE NECESSITIES OF LIFE

I've got a bookcase full of recipe books,
Though I never ever cook.
I have cupboards crammed with cleaning stuff
In every cranny, crack and nook.

I have clothes for each occasion,
My wardrobe starts to groan,
Though I prefer to be unsociable
And would rather stay at home.

I have hundreds of CDs
And DVDs by the score.
Too many to search for what I want,
So I go out and buy some more.

I have exercise equipment,
So that maybe on a whim,
I can make myself a little fitter
Without recourse to a gym.

I have notebooks, pens and paperclips
Of every shape and size,
Though they rarely leave the study,
Not to anyone's surprise.

My house is full to bursting,
No room for any more,
Though I can still see one small empty space
Right there upon the floor.

With all this useless hoarding,
You may think my brain has flipped,
But for most eventualities,
I'll be really well-equipped!

*****

THE CRASHING BORE

You've had an encounter just like this,
Of that I'm very sure.
You are the captive audience,
He is the crashing bore!

Whatever you say you have done
He's doubtless done it too,
But when he starts his diatribe
You feel you're stuck to him like glue.

You sit and nod and smile and say
"How interesting, I'm sure"
He's convinced his tale is riveting
And one his audience will adore.

You try to find some common ground,
But he doesn't give a damn.
You may be dancing on the ceiling,
But he's cycled in Vietnam.

You don't really need to listen,
He'll lecture you till you're bored,
And just when you think he's finished,
He'll start ranting off some more.

He has no sense of humour,
Whatever joke you choose.
And the fact that you exist at all,
Will leave him quite bemused.

Not content with the small things in life,
He writes his canvas large.
The war would not have happened,
If he had been in charge!

You'll find that you just can't escape,
He'll simply talk some more.
He's so engrossed, he just won't notice,
As you edge towards the door!

Now it's getting quite predictable.
Who's he think he's kidding?
When he starts: "But the interesting thing is this "
You know it really isn't!

He doesn't want your opinion,
There's only one course he can follow,
So just relax, let you mind run free
And dream of the joys to come tomorrow.

*****

AT A DINNER PARTY

Your knowledge is clearly outstanding,
Your achievements ahead of the game,
But in the ten seconds I've known you,
I've already forgotten your name!

*****

THE LONELY VOLUNTEER

I volunteer at the local museum,
It's very small and quaint,
And though I enjoy being busy,
Rushed off my feet, I definitely ain't.

I'm often the only person on duty,
But it's better than being at home,
Though if no-one comes to visit,
I end up sitting here all alone.

Knitting helps to wile away the hours,
If no-one else comes near.
And acquaintances, friends and relations,
Are given over-long scarves to wear!

I'm pleased to help the community;
I give my services free.
And I enjoy imparting the knowledge
That the public expect from me.

Local history is really so interesting.
People proudly claim this town for their birth.
And when some unsuspecting soul comes to visit
the museum,
I'll talk for all I am worth.

They may ask a simple question;
I can pad it out a treat.
And if they lose interest and wander off,
I've even followed them up the street!

On one quiet day, a man stopped by,
I almost pinned him to the wall,
But he only came to read the meters;
Didn't want my help at all!

Now they've decided to make me redundant;
Said they needed to make some cuts,
And installed these new whizz-bang computers;
Technology now is a must.

But the human touch is important;
Computers don't ooze sympathy.
And I helped make the visitors feel welcome.
Won't you please come and talk with me?

*****

THE BLUES

As I was walking down the road
A thought popped in my head:
How can I have the winter blues,
When I'm always seeing red?

FORGET PARIS

This week, I should've been in Paris,
But the tour company cancelled the trip.
After planning the sights I was going to see,
I now feel decidedly miffed!

But it's no use regretting lost pleasures,
This jaunt wasn't meant to be.
I'll just put expectations behind me,
And get on with the life that I lead.

So I'm home and I'm desperately trying
To forget that I should be in France,
But it seems every time I turn around,
Reminders wherever I glance.

I have scenes of Paris on my bathroom wall,
So when I step out of the shower,
I usually enjoy these black-and-white photos;
Face-to-face with the Eiffel Tower.

An American in Paris is on the TV,
Le Weekend is showing at the flicks,
And a friend has just mentioned Notre Dame,
Is there no escaping this?

I'm not going to let it depress me,
I'm trying to stay upbeat,
But instead of a leisurely stroll by the Seine,
I'm shopping in my local High Street.

The travel agent has posters of Paris.,
The bookshop has French guidebooks galore,
The gift shop has a cushion with a Parisian scene
on it.
I'd don't want reminding any more.

Just to rub in my disappointment further,
There's a French market in town today,
So I quickly have to try and dodge round that;
From this theme, there's no getting away.

There are stalls of bread and cheese and crepes,
The overpowering garlic smell is sweet,
And Françoise Hardy's *Chanson d'Amour,*
Has me singing down the street.

And I will go back to Paris,
Enjoy the cafés, gourmet food to eat,
And the art and architecture I adore -
Just don't keep rubbing it in this week!

OPEN TO THE PUBLIC

After visiting a country house on a very crowded bank holiday weekend, I wondered what the original owner might have thought about all these visitors!

I used to own a country house.
In the 1800s, I held sway,
But I'd find things very different now,
If I could see it all today.

The sheep and deer that used to roam
Freely over the estate,
Are now displaced by cars and coaches,
As they come flocking through the gates.

Visitors were always welcome,
But they came in twos and threes.
Now they're descending in their thousands
And there's hardly room to breathe.

My possessions have been catalogued,
All my knick-knacks have been labelled,
Where once my home was lived-in,
Now there are antiques on the tables.

It seems so artificial;
It's not like real life.
More a place to entertain the kids
Or stroll round with the wife.

My hospitality was legion;
Guests were never urged to rush.
Now ticket holders are shuffled through
And entreated not to touch.

I was renowned for lavish parties,
The servants worked so hard,
Now its sandwiches in the conservatory
And ice-creams in the yard.

My visitors had some decorum,
They might even put on airs,
But now the people dress in trainers
And mustn't sit upon the chairs.

My friends were made to feel at ease;
To my generosity, no end,
But now there's the ever-present gift shop,
To encourage visitors to spend.

I used to show my guests around;
Describe my treasures, with such pride.
Now they have their noses in their guidebooks
And play the game, *I-Spy*!

They are wandering through my parlour,
They are tramping through my loo,
And commenting on the distant past
And what they think I used to do.

It's become almost Disney-like;
A re-creation of a different age,
With not much link to real life;
More like scenery on a stage.

So what has been achieved here?
A tableau built to last?
Things preserved in aspic
As a semblance of the past?

Or just a kind of theme park
For kids on a Sunday afternoon.
Or a way of raking in money
To preserve a giant big balloon!

*****

THE TOUR GUIDE

I'm your friendly tour guide,
You may think that I look thick,
But the regular tour guide
Suddenly phoned in sick!

I'll do my best to entertain you,
Show you round the house and garden.
My knowledge is not extensive
And for that I beg your pardon.

Though I have a passion for this place,
Insight have I none.
I may not be an expert,
But at least I'll make it fun!

I coat my face in make-up –
It took me such an age.
My delivery may be stilted,
But I'll pretend I'm on the stage.

This is lovely, that it lovely,
Interesting too,
But ask me any questions
And I haven't got a clue!

I can read the odd description;
I have the guide book close to hand
And I'll fill out my shortcomings
With gestures over-grand.

The house is so historical,
And I can play mine host.
You may disagree with what I tell you,
But it says so in my notes!

I'll show you round the garden,
Point out the obvious things to see.
I don't know what I'm talking about,
But I can quote a fact or three.

It's a lovely location;
Lots of landscapes one can choose,
So when the film crew came along,
I told them what to do.

My reading may be boring
And I may just start to stutter.
If you can't catch all I'm saying,
Please don't interrupt me with a mutter.

You may not've learnt much history,
But you have been entertained,
And I've put on such a wondrous show,
You'll want to come again.

Now the highlight of the tour is coming,
The thing you should not forget.
There's tea and cake in the ballroom,
So you won't want to leave just yet!

*****

MARBLES

The owner of a stately pile
Went out one day, for quite a while
And left unlocked, all unbeknown,
The front door of his noble home.

An opportunist thief passed by,
His luck was in, to boot,
He strolled inside and helped himself,
Then carted off his loot.

The squire returned home later
And looking round his castle,
To his despair, the hall was bare,
He found he'd lost his marbles!

*****

THE TRAVELLING BUG

I'm a recurring 'travaholic'
Feeling somewhat melancholic,
Just returned from holiday and settled in at
home.
But with travel thoughts still reeling
And hopes still clinging to the ceiling,
I know it won't be long before I get the itch
again to roam.

Once more I'll be off travelling,
Before my plans all start unravelling,
With fantastic sights ahead that lead me to
explore.
For the brochures keep on coming
And are well-tattered from the thumbing,
So before too long, I'll find I've booked another
tour!

There are still so many undiscovered places
And time really seems to race as
I frantically try and travel to excess.
For while the body may be willing
And I've money for the billing,
I just don't have the time to sit and rest.

Though as the days grow ever longer,
And my wandering days are numbered,
Brief respites at home may turn to longer stays.
By then I may have lost my curiosity,
As my body starts to struggle for velocity,
And I'll console myself with memories from
happier days.

*****

A WANDERING MIND

I long to go exploring
And see exciting places.
I would love to be adventurous
And kick away the traces.

All those enterprising women,
Travelling alone.
I really want to emulate
The courage they have shown.

How marvellous to wend my way
Through undiscovered lands;
To talk with other cultures,
Traverse the shifting sands.

The orient looks so exotic,
Behold its many charms,
But the reality of travelling there,
Somehow starts to ring alarms.

I love the thought of sailing solo
Across the seven seas,
But the vast expanse of sea and sky,
Leaves me shaking at the knees.

Oh, the romance of the desert
Viewed from a camel's hump,
Though in real life I'd be falling off,
Landing ungainly, in a lump.

I could hack my way through jungle,
Dressed in a pith hat and a sari,
But the thought of treading on a snake,
Is scary and alarming.

Then there's the bandits and the brigands,
The pirates and the thieves;
There's really so much danger,
To dent the confidence I feel.

The polar regions also beckon,
Though the cold's a disadvantage,
And the ice just keeps on drifting,
So I don't think I will chance it.

The challenge of raw nature,
How romantic it all seems,
But I love my comforts far too much,
Maybe I'll just stay home and dream.

*****

VENICE

Had a lovely time in Venice,
The buildings were a treat,
But just one tiny problem -
I couldn't walk across the street!

*****

THE HOLIDAY TWIST

I love to travel round the world,
Fly away to a tropical island.
I could hike in Nepal,
Go anywhere, have a ball:
America, Australia or Thailand.

My cleaner has gone to the Isle of Wight;
I wouldn't begrudge her the trip,
For I don't make a fuss,
As she's clearing the dust
And I'll pick up the pieces she's missed.

My electrician has changed all my light fittings.
With his invoice, there's not much that's free.
Now are my wires crossed
Or has the plot just been lost?
For he's taken himself to 'Paree' .

My handyman holidays in the Med these days.
He fixed all my gutters with glee.
On the strength of the bill,
His friend went as well,
While I'm funding this nice little spree!

My plumber can't fix my loo right now;
He's in Hawaii and I'm feeling peeved,
But he'll come and attack
The leak at the back,
When he's home from indefinite leave.

My builder charges an arm and a leg,
So he holidays in the Azores.
He has just cut and run,
Left my extension half done.
When he comes back, he'll bill me for more.

My travelling days may be numbered.
No more exotic places I'll roam.
Having paid all this lot,
No more cash in the pot,
So I'll end up just staying at home.

*****

THE SUITCASE

With four wheels on my suitcase
It's easy to roll it along,
But make no mistakes
For without any brakes
Let it go, on a slope, and it's gone
        . . . . rapidly disappearing downhill!!!

THE RELUCTANT TOURIST

We went on a cultural holiday,
To explore a foreign land.
It was supposed to be an adventure,
But it didn't turn out how we planned.

The flight was entertaining,
On the coach we had a lovely ride.
The hotel looks just wonderful,
But then we had to step outside!

I know the sights are all out there,
But do we have to take a look?
They'll still be there tomorrow
Or we can see them in a book.

I know we're supposed to see the monuments,
But it's such a crashing bore,
Though the tour guide's enthusiastic,
And wants to show us more.

We thought it would be quite easy:
The odd gallery or museum to view,
But there's miles and miles to tramp around,
Outside and inside too.

Slow slow quick quick slow:
It's the tourist shuffle and away we go.
Eyes cast down, dragging the feet,
Following blindly, stagger down the street.

The weather was a problem:
Pelting with rain or much too hot,
And we forgot the brolly and the sunscreen.
Must we do the blinking lot?

No-one spoke any English;
You'd have thought that at least they'd try.
They must realise they are 'foreigners',
At least through these strangers' eyes.

Can we go back to the hotel now?
Spend the evening on our own.
It would be much more comfortable,
And we'll pretend that we're at home.

We came to explore the city.
We came to be entertained.
It wasn't our fault, that we hardly went out
And that every day it rained.

You have to see this, you have to see that;
The paintings and sculptures are a must.
And we'll bore you to tears with the photos,
Before the memories all fade to dust.

We went on a cultural holiday.
Exhausted, we took to our bed.
And we won't be going back again;
Next time we'll sit on the beach instead.

*****

THE UMBRELLA

I lent someone my umbrella,
Not really very sure why.
She held it aloft,
Then turned around, to my cost,
And almost poked out my eye!

I then passed the umbrella to someone else.
How much more virtuous could I get?
She held it on high,
Used it well to keep dry,
And then handed it back to me . . . . wet!

THE VISITOR

It's great to have a visitor
Someone to come and stay,
Though it's really so much harder
To get them to go away!

I said "Come for a few nights"
And she said "Oh, yes please",
Now how can I broach the subject
Of when she's going to leave?

She's settled in quite nicely
Got her feet under the table
And doesn't seem inclined to help,
In spite of being able.

I mumble about appointments
That I really have to keep,
But she says "Just you go ahead.
I'm fine here, don't mind me".

I say she must be missing home
And what about the cat?
But she doesn't seem all that concerned
As a neighbour deals with that.

She said she'd take me out to dine
But when it came to pay,
She found she'd left her purse at 'home'
Or at least in my hallway.

Maybe she's too comfortable here;
I'm much too good a host.
If I start dropping hints around,
Then maybe she would go.

Sometime soon I may well crack
And when the time is right,
I'll throw all her belongings
Out the window, in the night.

And when she does decide to leave
"It's all your fault" she'd say
"I would have left some days ago,
But I knew you wanted me to stay"!

*****

TRAVELLING

I travel very light these days
One small suitcase, as you see . . . .
Plus the 27 others
With the extras I might need!

REVENGE OF THE SAT. NAV.

I always rely on my sat nav
It's like having a friend in the car,
And if I should stray from my usual way,
She most often knows where we are.

My sat nav's name is Winnie;
I've discovered who is the boss,
'Cos if I don't do what she tells me,
She's liable to get really cross.

" *Turn around when possible*" -
Words I've come to anticipate,
Though if I don't follow directions,
She'll grudgingly recalculate.

Sometimes Winnie likes to tease me
On a journey from A to B,
By ducking and diving down country lanes,
Her logic is hard to see,

When a couple of easy main roads
Would've taken me a much simpler way.
Do you think she's set on retaliation
For my disobedience on a previous day?

Though when I got lost at Heathrow,
I couldn't believe what I'd seen,
For the road in front of my very eyes,
Bore no resemblance to what was on her screen!

Maybe she wanted to teach me a lesson;
It was worrying for a short time,
Though as soon as I recognized where I was,
She helpfully came back on line!

But I can take my own revenge.
I'm determined to get the last laugh,
For if she decides to get too cocky,
I'll reach out and just switch her off!

On the whole, she's incredibly useful,
Avoiding traffic where I might get stuck.
I appreciate the help that she gives me,
Instead of just trusting to luck.

I'll conclude this by thanking dear Winnie.
Despite her faults, I'll stick with her to the end,
So she'll take me wherever I want to go,
Instead of driving me straight round the bend!

*****

THE JOYS OF GETTING OLDER

As I'm getting older
Sometimes I just don't have the heart,
And it's becoming increasingly obvious,
That things are starting to fall apart!

My knees have started creaking
And when I drop things on the floor,
I don't bend down as quickly
As I used to do before.

My hair is definitely thinner
And turning white as well.
It used to have some colour,
But now that's very hard to tell.

My teeth have started cracking
And the crowns have all dropped out.
Now hot air can circulate
Between the gaps inside my mouth.

Don't want another back spasm;
My muscles feel they're hardening,
But that may be just excuses
To get out of the gardening?

My body's started drooping
Though I'm loathe to tell you where.
I was so lithe and nimble,
But now I flop down in a chair.

I may nod off in a lecture,
As my concentration wanes.
My mind wanders as I read a book,
I'll have to read that page again.

I can't remember all the things
That I once used to do,
And all the things you told me recently,
I just don't have a clue.

I need a list to remind me,
Of the tasks to do today,
But where on earth did I put that list?
I had it yesterday.

Now I'm starting to get tetchy.
My patience grows quite thin.
Never mind the tonic,
Just pour me one more gin!

*****

BITS AND PIECES

My body's served me very well,
But now I don't feel quite so fit.
I need a few improvements
And could use some artificial bits!

Looks are so important;
Contact lenses are for me,
So all the people that I meet,
Can't see that I can't see!

My teeth no longer sparkle,
Like when I was a child,
But with my gleaming set of dentures,
I can once more flash a smile.

Some micro-electronic wizardry
Is now plugged into my ear,
So I can listen in to conversations,
That I may not want to hear.

With this brand new hearing aid,
Things seem so much clearer now to me,
And on a really quiet day,
I can pick up Radio Three!

It's very reassuring,
What medical science can do.
Now my joints are held together
With bolts and plates and screws.

The metal in my replacement hip,
Works just like a charm,
Except when I'm near security
And it triggers the alarms!

All these expensive artificial aids,
Are definitely helping my endurance,
But I may have to pay a hefty premium,
For bodily insurance.

I'd like to thank the doctors,
For the gadgets they've made for me.
Now instead of one more medical,
I'll book myself an M.O.T.!

And thank you to the technicians,
They are really very clever,
So just to get my money's worth,
I plan to live forever!

*****

ODE TO A LOST FRIEND

It's less than an hour
Till I'm due at the dentist.
I'm having a tooth pulled
And I rather resent it.

This friend who has served me
For fifty odd years,
In an hour will be history
And have just 'disappeared'.

It's chewed and it's chomped
Through thousands of meals,
And to cast it aside,
How ungrateful that feels.

After days and hours of worry,
The dreaded time is here,
And it's all over in ten minutes;
You'd think I'd be ready to cheer.

But like any old faithful companion,
We've shared in some good times and strife,
And without the old tooth in its preordained
place,
There's a definite gap in my life.

So did I preserve the sad remnant,
Evermore to reflect on this stash?
No, I left it there in the surgery,
To be thrown away with the trash!

*****

TOE WHOM IT MAY CONCERN

I'm in absolute agony
But I'm keeping on the go,
Hobbling around like a hundred year old,
With a very painful toe.

But no-one wants to listen,
To this dreadful tale of woe
There's really nothing they can see;
'*What a fuss over just one toe*!'

A black eye, there for all to see,
Elicits such great sympathy,
But just because it doesn't show,
My injury seems to be incognito[e].

Crutches might get some attention,
While plaster casts and slings all show.
Though no-one gives a second thought,
To my hidden little toe.

Why do other people's injuries
Always seem more glamorous?
While mine are always so mundane:
'*I slipped when I was in the rain*'.

Others tell their stories in such detail,
It all seems so heroical.
My toe is just as painful,
But I have to be more stoical.

What about '*My neighbour's cat climbed up a
tree*
And needed certain rescue.
Like Superwoman, there I am
Determined now to be successful.

'*The branch began to swing and sway,*
Disaster struck as I came down.
The cat, uninjured, ran away,
While I came crashing to the ground.'

Or '*It was while I was in the Arctic*',
Is that really inconceivable?
'*And frostbite is so painful*',
Maybe that is slightly more believable?

'*I stubbed my toe in the bathroom*'.
I know it's a lame excuse,
But of all the other options,
This one's closer to the truth.

So if you do yourself an injury,
Make sure it's one that shows,
Then ham it up for all it's worth,
So everybody knows . . .

. . . that you're suffering in 'silence',
You're not one to make a fuss,
But just require a bit of TLC
And an awful lot of sympathy.

*****

CHURNING ON THE INSIDE

I may look easy going
But what you may not guess:
On the outside, all is ordered
On the inside, I'm a mess!

There's a maelstrom churning in my head,
I'll admit it if you press me,
As each new experience
Seems destined to distress me.

In a strange new situation
I can stride into the place,
Trying hard to stop the look of terror
From appearing on my face.

In a social encounter
I may feel positively demented,
Though I can eke out friendly conversation
And act as if I really meant it.

I may appear to stay quite calm
If I am forced to wait,
But beneath this cool exterior
I panic that I'm late.

The calmness and the placidness
Are just a total bluff,
For my brain is in a turmoil
As it wants to run amok.

So don 't be fooled by the person
Who outwardly seems charming.
The muddled state of their affairs
Can sometimes prove alarming.

By putting two and two together
One may end up with three,
As we try to figure out
How everyone else appears to be.

READY FOR THE SIEGE

The weatherman says that it's coming
The coldest snap of the year,
So I need to get myself organised
Put emergency plans into gear.

I'm prepared for the really cold weather.
I've stocked up for when it is bleak.
I have everything in my store cupboard,
Though I'm making more lists as we speak.

I won't go out if the pavement is icy,
Not even to 'slip' to the stores.
I've enough supplies for an army
Or at least till the icicles thaw.

I have stacks of food in the freezer.
I've got baked beans and soup in tins
And snacks galore, crisps by the score.
I'm sure I won't starve staying in.

I have salt for the path, spray for the car
And one of those handy snow shovels,
So if all else fails and I'm snowed in one day,
I can dig myself out of trouble.

I have hats and scarves, snow boots and wellies,
Thermals and fleeces in store
And grippers for shoes, and waterproofs too.
Could I want for anything more?

If I order online, I can get more supplies
And someone else will bring 'em
And if I can't meet, friends I usually greet,
I can pick up the phone and ring 'em.

The internet's there to amuse me.
I've piles of books ready to read.
If there's nothing good on the telly,
I'll resort to some old DVDs.

Though we may be subject to power cuts
In which case I'll twiddle my thumbs.
I have bottles of wine, to wile away time
By candlelight, eating up crumbs.

You may think I'm crazy to stock up like mad,
When the shops are just down the street,
But I'll be the hero, when the temperature's
zero,
Helping neighbours, stuck in just like me.

If the snow and the ice doesn't hit us
And the forecasters made a mistake,
At least I'm prepared for the next time
And I may not have that long to wait . . .

DIETING IS EASY

I don't need to diet
I'm really not that fat
But my spare tyre is inflating
And I'm not too thrilled with that.

All I need is to give up food,
I could easily get the knack;
Starve myself throughout the day
And reward myself with a snack.

Everyone has good advice:
They said I should watch what I ate,
So instead of consuming all the food
I stared at it on the plate.

Dieting is easy
All it takes is willpower
And a carrot and some lettuce
Might keep me going a whole hour.

Dieting is easy
Just try and stand your ground.
Remember that the extra grape
Could put on half a pound.

To get a sylph-like body
Is maybe wishful thinking,
Though the effort that it would entail
Might lead me towards drinking.

It's just a case of give and take:
I could easily give up wine,
Though I'll keep a bottle on the shelf
To sip from time to time.

I comb the High Street for what to eat:
Healthy 'sallard', fresh 'baggets'.*
Do these incorrect spellings
Indicate the calories are less?

Dieting is depressing
I'll need some comfort food,
Munch my way through crisps and chocs,
Then really start to brood.

So factor in some exercise,
The healthy life for me.
I'll take a good long power walk,
Then stop for cakes and tea.

Dieting is just a myth.
If you need to be alluring
Just eat a little less each day
Though that is, frankly . . . boring!

THE ART OF CONVERSATION

Two friends sit next to one another
But they've nothing much to say,
Though they text each other frequently
And email every day.

The art of conversation
Has quietly died, I fear,
For the invention of technology
Makes it all abundantly clear . . .

. . . that we can no longer communicate
The old-fashioned way, face to face.
Now our inbuilt inhibitions
Can be hidden in cyberspace.

Social media has taken over,
Social graces are no more.
Say "Good morning" to a computer
And your credibility hits the floor.

Go into a supermarket,
Check out with a machine.
Step into your friendly bank
And face a maze of screens.

No need to talk to anyone;
Take no notice anyway.
The silent whirr is deafening
And information slips away.

Though today I chatted to a stranger;
Inconsequential ramblings were said.
So maybe conversation as we used to know it,
Is not entirely dead . . . . . !!!

*****

BALLROOM DANCING

*Reflections after a visit
to the Tower Ballroom, Blackpool.*

It's eleven o'clock in the morning,
They've come for coffee, out of the rain,
But suddenly spirits are lifted,
As the Wurlitzer starts to play.

They feel rather cautious and nervous,
Leading each other out on the floor.
He takes her hand, they step forward,
Into the limelight once more.

They may not want to be first on the dance
floor.
Should someone else lead the way?
But as they step into the spotlight,
Their cares are just melted away.

They're an ordinary couple,
They have worries and woes by the score,
But their problems all evaporate,
As they step on to the magic dance floor.

His paunch is quietly forgotten.
She stands straight as if lifted by strings.
They lock hands and move to the music,
Hearts have suddenly taken on wings.

They're no longer the old retired couple,
Now they're so much younger than they feel.
In real life they may be Darby and Joan
But for now they're Torvill and Dean.

And the music lifts them ever upwards,
They are gradually transported away.
They're lifted on shoulders of giants,
As they join with the rest of the fray.

They are wearing their t-shirts and trainers,
But with the magic of all they behold,
They appear in their sequins and black ties,
Swirling round in this circle of gold.

For dreams are the stuff of this ballroom.
He whirls her across the dance floor
And just for a moment, they're living in heaven,
In each other's embrace so secure.

They waltz to the music of Gershwin,
They tango for all they are worth,
For five minutes they dance in their glory,
Until they come back down to earth.

And though I'm on the side-lines and watching,
And tapping my foot to the beat,
For one small moment, I'm with them,
Envying their brief time of release.

*****

BAD BACK

I had a bad back, so I went to the store
To buy ointment to help myself,
But I had to come home with nothing,
For they were all on the lowest shelf!

*****

HOW ARE YOU TODAY?

A chance encounter on the street,
Out of politeness I may say:
"How's the world been treating you?"
Or "How are you today?"

It's just a casual enquiry;
I don't need to have a list
Of all the aches and pains and niggles,
With exact descriptions of every bit.

And the operation that you had -
Oh isn't life a bore!
Though you revel in the minutiae
Of all the blood and gore.

I wish I hadn't asked at all;
It was just a friendly note
And I may appear sympathetic
But I'm not that keen to know.

So if I ask about your health,
Just mumble a quick "Okay"
And I'll reply the same to you in passing
And we can head off on our way.

*****

JENNIFER GREEN

TOO MUCH INFORMATION

It's a disease that's happening everywhere
It's all across the nation,
As every company and business
Wants to give us too much information.

The banks and the insurance firms
Thrive on the small print,
But when the print gets even smaller,
I begin to take the hint

That they don't want us to read it all;
The paperless society is a myth
And I want to go back to the good old days
Of not needing to know what everything is.

And the price comparisons and insurance sites
Which claim to save you money,
Leave me more confused than ever
And I'm running home for cover.

The advice is don't sign anything
Till you've read all the small print.
In that case I won't sign at all
And that will cause a stink.

Maybe I should start a trend
And write my own conditions;
If they had to comply with all my terms
Then they might just take the hint
                    . . . . (though I doubt it!).

But in reality, it's sobering
That we sign our lives away,
Without any comprehension
Of what documents really say.

So when I need to make decisions
And I don't understand the flow,
I ask an 'expert' what to do
And hope to hell he knows.

*****

NEW YEAR'S RESOLUTION

I made a New Year's resolution
There's not much more to say.
Then I stuck to it rigidly
For almost one whole day!

*****

NOW IS THE TIME

Now I've reached a certain age,
I think it's time to rant and rage.
No longer standing on the side-lines,
I'll opt for centre stage.

Now's the time for confrontation,
Put my opinions before the nation.
Time to make my feelings clear,
Not sit back and say "Oh dear"!

The world has changed since I was young
(My parents sang this same old song)
But now the kids all Tweet and Twitter.
So I'll go home and write a letter.

Mobile phones are all around,
One can't avoid the dreadful sound
Of someone shouting to explain
"I'll be late home. I'm on the train"!

We must cry out and right all wrongs
With signed petitions, protest songs.
And say exactly what we mean,
Go out now and make a scene.

So into battle we will go,
Charging forward as we must
And I'll be there with you in spirit,
Though you won't see me for dust!

*****

THE INVITATION – PART ONE

Oh, I wish she hadn't asked me.
Now I'll really have to go.
Too late to make excuses
Or contemplate 'no show'.

If I'd had time to think about it,
Could have said "I'd love to, but . . . "
And then found a way out somehow,
Without making too much fuss.

There'll be no-one that I know there
And they'll all be dressed to kill.
My tiara's packed in mothballs
And I'm starting to feel ill.

There'll be no-one I can talk to,
And they'll all know one another;
If only I could disappear
Or use the drapes for cover.

There'll be nothing I can eat there
And if I drive there, I can't drink,
But's it's too late to get out of it;
It would cause an awful stink.

And I'd hate to spoil a friendship,
Appear standoffish, saying 'no',
But it's getting near the dreaded date
And I just don't want to go.

Now is the time for leaving home.
Will I get held up on the way?
Should I be late or early?
And what on earth am I to say?

And now I push the doorbell;
It's much too late to run.
But the evening is delightful
And I'm so glad that I've come!

*****

THE INVITATION – PART TWO

Oh, I wish I hadn't asked her:
"Come for coffee, just pop round"
As the words came flying out my mouth
I'm listening to the sound!

It's just a chat and coffee,
An hour or two at most.
Why get myself all worked up,
If I'm not the world's best host.

But I'm not used to entertaining;
So much happier on my own.
It's my own fault for inviting her -
Try to stifle one huge groan.

I could forget the appointment
And muddle things about,
To find that she was popping in,
As I was popping out.

I try to keep the place quite clean
And though it's not a must,
If I thought pops quickly in my head,
I can write it in the dust!

If I tidy up completely
And put everything away,
I'll never find what I want, where I want it,
When I want it now, like yesterday.

Does she drink regular or decaff,
Or would she prefer tea,
Or maybe something stronger
With the shock of seeing me?

And will she expect biscuits,
Or I'll buy a piece of cake;
Inedible if I baked it,
So I won't make that mistake.

Will she want to take her coat off?
When did I last clean the loo?
There's only one day left to go
And a million things to do!

I know that I'm neurotic,
What more can I say?
And this is just one cup of coffee,
Not like she's come to stay.

As the hour grows ever nearer,
There must be some take and give
And when she's here, she'll have to see
This is just the way I live.

Well I'm ready now and waiting;
Pace the carpet, relive all my fears
And I swear I won't invite anyone ever
For years, and years, and years.

So if I'm stupid and I ask you,
Don't pretend you've somewhere to go;
No need to make excuses,
Look me straight in the eye and say "No"!

THE END OF LIFE [but not quite yet!]

Well, you've had it now you're sixty;
There's nothing left to do.
Just sit and wait for the years to pass
And then roll on . . . 62

You're turning into your mother,
Better join the W.I.
Don't let future years of jam-making
Fritter and pass you by.

And you could sing *Jerusalem,*
If you only knew the words
And weren't completely tone deaf
And could make yourself be heard!

And then there is the U3A,
On which your brain can feed
And learn a hundred languages,
That you'll never ever need.

Order the Zimmer frame early:
High-flying, state-of-the-art,
Though when you finally need it,
It'll look like a creaking cart.

Or get an electric scooter
Go careering round the town,
Playing the game of nine-pins
Knocking all the pedestrians down!

You've surely got the message -
Life ain't all full of tricks,
But it's better than the bucket
That you never want to kick!

*****

THE PUNCH LINE

I've searched every dictionary,
Rhymed every rhyme,
But I just can't quite figure,
That elusive punch-line.

I can churn out the verses,
But it drives me round the bend.
I need a suitable punch-line,
To know when the end . . . is the end.

*****

Made in the USA
Charleston, SC
26 February 2015